# GARFIELD
## IN PARADISE

BY: JIM DAVIS

BALLANTINE BOOKS • NEW YORK

Copyright © 1986 by United Feature Syndicate, Inc. GARFIELD IN PARADISE is based on the television special produced by United Media Productions. Jay Poynor, Executive Producer, in association with Lee Mendelson and Phil Roman. Created by Jim Davis. Designed by Gary Barker © 1986 United Feature Syndicate, Inc. All rights reserved under International and Pan-American Copyright Conventions. Published in the United States by Ballantine Books, a division of Random House, Inc., New York, and simultaneously in Canada by Random House of Canada Limited, Toronto

Library of Congress Catalog Card Number: 86-90759

ISBN: 0-345-33796-4

Manufactured in the United States of America

First Edition: May 1986

20   19   18   17   16   15

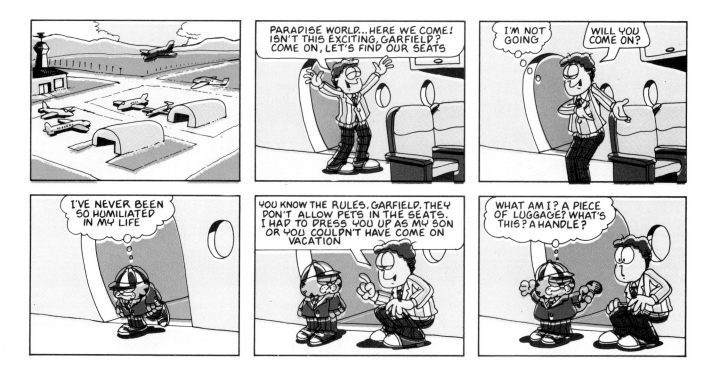

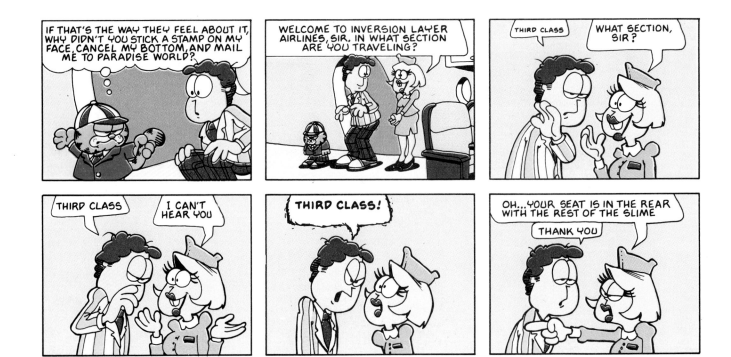

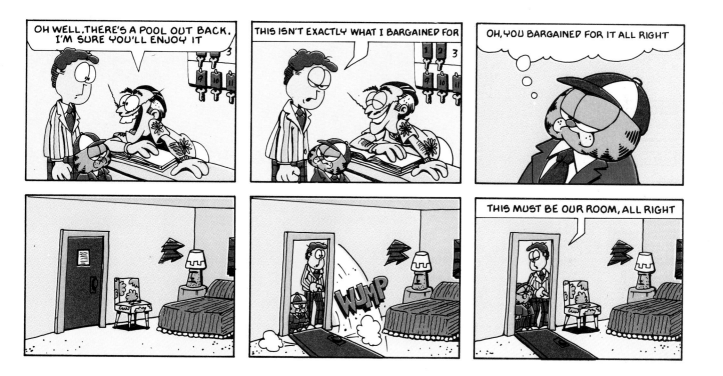

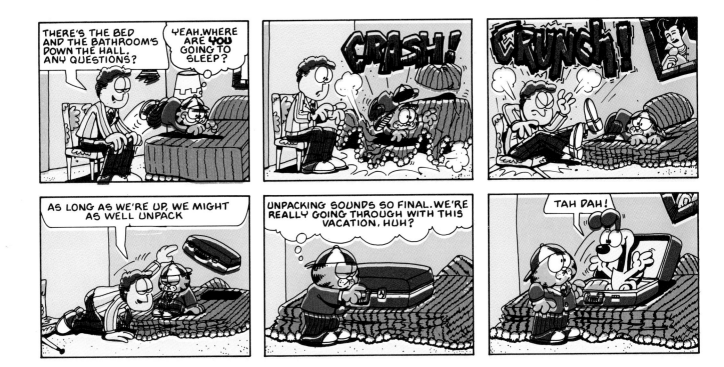

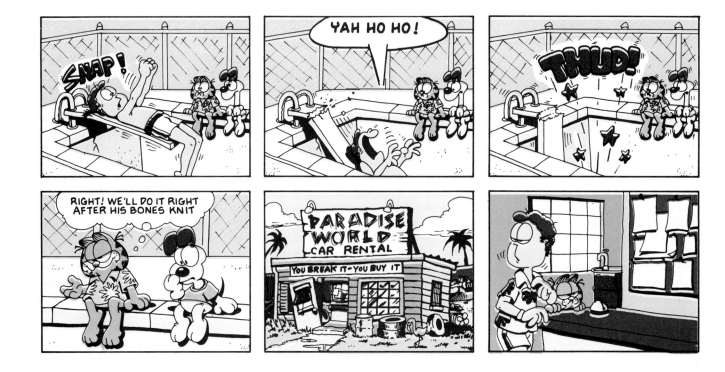

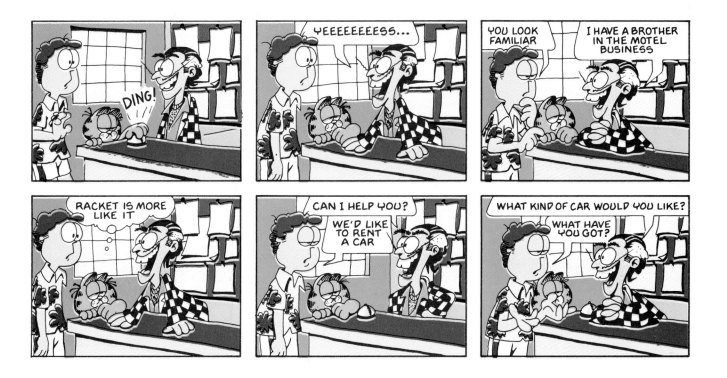

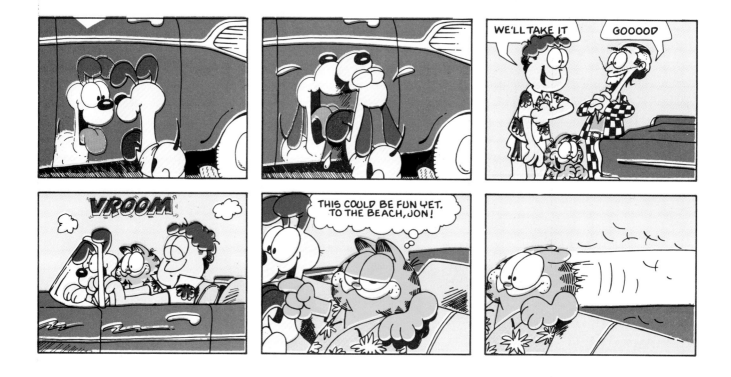

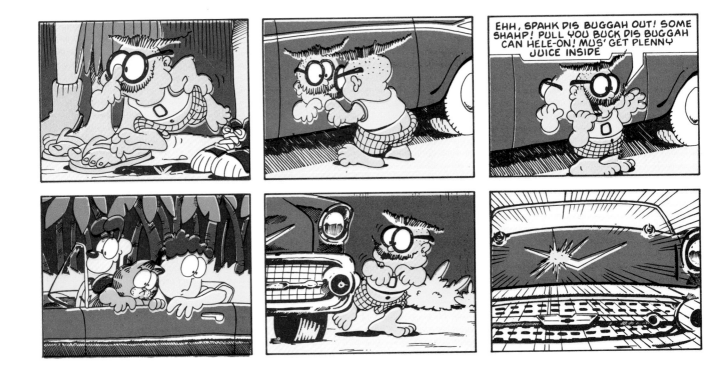

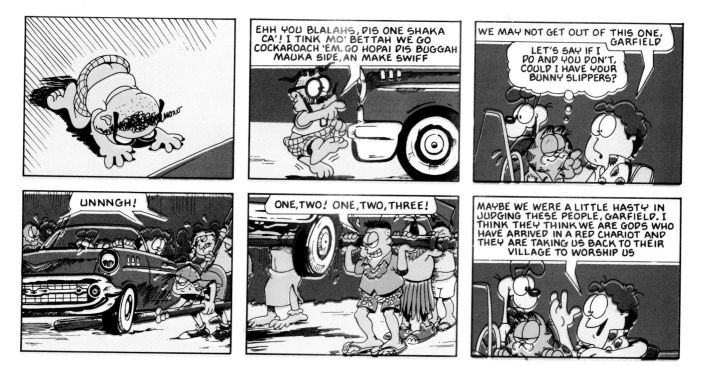

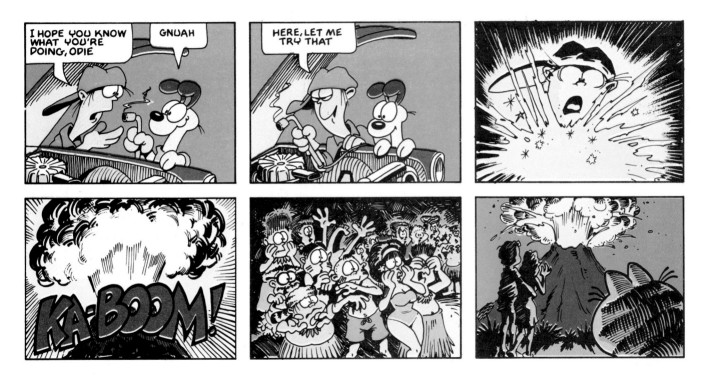

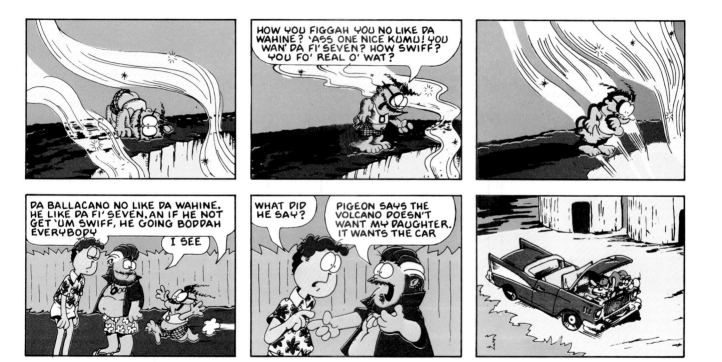

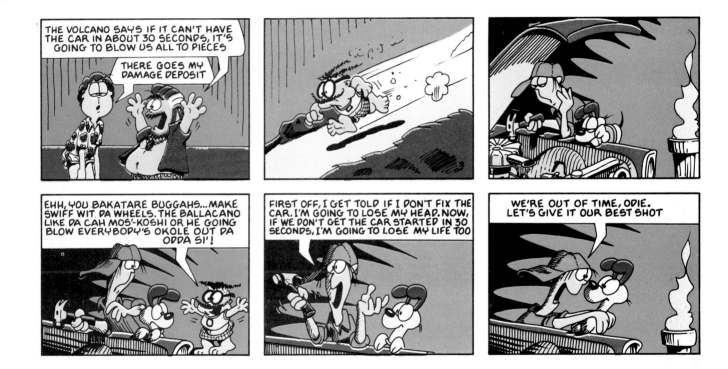

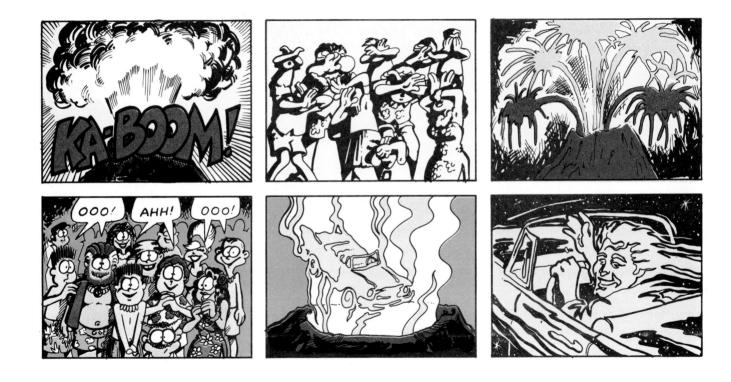

# BIRTHDAYS, HOLIDAYS, OR ANY DAY . . .

*Keep GARFIELD on your calendar all year 'round!*

**GARFIELD TV SPECIALS**
__BABES & BULLETS     36339/$6.95
__A GARFIELD CHRISTMAS     34368/$6.95
__GARFIELD GOES HOLLYWOOD     34580/$6.95
__GARFIELD'S HALLOWEEN ADVENTURE     33045/$6.95
  (formerly GARFIELD In Disguise)
__GARFIELD'S FELINE FANTASIES     36903/$6.95
__GARFIELD IN PARADISE     33796/$6.95
__GARFIELD IN THE ROUGH     32242/$6.95
__GARFIELD ON THE TOWN     31542/$6.95
__A GARFIELD THANKSGIVING     35650/$6.95
__HERE COMES GARFIELD     32012/$6.95

BALLANTINE SALES
Dept. TA, 201 E. 50th St., New York, N.Y. 10022

Please send me the BALLANTINE BOOKS I have checked above. I am enclosing $ ................ (add $2.00 for the first book and 50¢ for each additional book to cover postage and handling). Send check or money order—no cash or C.O.D.'s please. Prices are subject to change without notice.

**GREETINGS FROM GARFIELD!**
GARFIELD POSTCARD BOOKS FOR ALL OCCASIONS.
__#1 THINKING OF YOU     36516/$6.95
__#2 WORDS TO LIVE BY     36679/$6.95
__#3 GARFIELD BIRTHDAY GREETINGS     36770/$7.95
__#4 BE MY VALENTINE     37121/$7.95

**Also from GARFIELD:**
__GARFIELD: HIS NINE LIVES     32061/$9.95
__THE GARFIELD BOOK OF CAT NAMES     35082/$5.95
__THE GARFIELD TRIVIA BOOK     33771/$5.95
__THE UNABRIDGED UNCENSORED
  UNBELIEVABLE GARFIELD     33772/$5.95
__GARFIELD: THE ME BOOK     36545/$7.95
__GARFIELD'S JUDGMENT DAY     36755/$6.95

Name_____

Address_____

City_____ State_____ Zip Code_____
30          Allow at least 4 weeks for delivery          3/90 TA-267

# STRIPS, SPECIALS OR BESTSELLING BOOKS . . . GARFIELD'S ON EVERYONE'S MENU

## Don't miss even one episode in the Tubby Tabby's hilarious series!

__GARFIELD AT LARGE (#1)   32013/$6.95
__GARFIELD GAINS WEIGHT (#2)   32008/$6.95
__GARFIELD BIGGER THAN LIFE (#3)   32007/$6.95
__GARFIELD WEIGHS IN (#4)   32010/$6.95
__GARFIELD TAKES THE CAKE (#5)   32009/$6.95
__GARFIELD EATS HIS HEART OUT (#6)   32018/$6.95
__GARFIELD SITS AROUND THE HOUSE (#7)   32011/$6.95
__GARFIELD TIPS THE SCALES (#8)   33580/$6.95
__GARFIELD LOSES HIS FEET (#9)   31805/$6.95
__GARFIELD MAKES IT BIG (#10)   31928/$6.95
__GARFIELD ROLLS ON (#11)   32634/$6.95
__GARFIELD OUT TO LUNCH (#12)   33118/$6.95
__GARFIELD FOOD FOR THOUGHT (#13)   34129/$6.95

__GARFIELD SWALLOWS HIS PRIDE (#14)   34725/$6.95
__GARFIELD WORLDWIDE (#15)   35158/$6.95
__GARFIELD ROUNDS OUT (#16)   35388/$6.95
__GARFIELD CHEWS THE FAT (#17)   35956/$6.95
__GARFIELD GOES TO WAIST (#18)   36430/$6.95
__GARFIELD HANGS OUT (#19)   36835/$6.95
__GARFIELD TAKES UP SPACE (#20)   37029/$6.95
__GARFIELD SAYS A MOUTHFUL (#21)   37368/$6.95
__GARFIELD BY THE POUND (#22)   37579/$6.95
__GARFIELD KEEPS HIS CHINS UP (#23)   37959/$6.95
__GARFIELD TAKES HIS LICKS (#24)   38170/$6.95
__GARFIELD HITS THE BIG TIME (#25)   38332/$6.95

**GARFIELD AT HIS SUNDAY BEST!**
__GARFIELD TREASURY   32106/$11.95
__THE SECOND GARFIELD TREASURY   33276/$10.95
__THE THIRD GARFIELD TREASURY   32635/$11.00
__THE FOURTH GARFIELD TREASURY   34726/$10.95
__THE FIFTH GARFIELD TREASURY   36268/$12.00
__THE SIXTH GARFIELD TREASURY   37367/$10.95
__THE SEVENTH GARFIELD TREASURY   38427/$10.95

Please send me the BALLANTINE BOOKS I have checked above. I am enclosing $_____. (Please add $2.00 for the first book and $.50 for each additional book for postage and handling and include the appropriate state sales tax.) Send check or money order (no cash or C.O.D.'s) to Ballantine Mail Sales Dept. TA, 400 Hahn Road, Westminster, MD 21157.

To order by phone, call 1-800-733-3000 and use your major credit card.

Prices and numbers are subject to change without notice. Valid in the U.S. only. All orders are subject to availability.

Name_____

Address_____

City_____ State_____ Zip_____

30                    Allow at least 4 weeks for delivery                    7/93